Books of related interest

Aids to Talmud Study by *Aryeh Carmell*
New, fourth edition, includes carefully revised sections of key Gemara words and phrases, in vocalized Aramaic with English translation; commonly used abbreviations explained and translated into English; a concise survey of Aramaic (Talmudic) grammar, and chronological charts of Tannaim and Amoraim. This expanded new edition adds the first English translation of Rabbi Samuel HaNagid's *Introduction to the Talmud* and tables of Talmudic weights and measures.

The Oral Law, by *H. Chaim Schimmel*
The Rabbinic contribution to *Torah sheb'al peh*, seen through the entire spectrum of the *halachah*. An attempt to answer some of the questions pertaining to the classical Jewish literature and the writings of the great, recognized Rabbinical authorities. A refreshing approach by a lifelong student of the Talmud.

The Student's Guide through the Talmud, by *Zvi Hirsch Chajes*
Translated from his classic *Mevo haTalmud*, edited and annotated by *Rabbi Dr Jacob Schachter*. This renowned work delineates the nature, extent and authority of Talmudic tradition, in the realms of both *halachah* and *aggadah*. The entire development and system of the Oral Law are made clear for the ordinary (non-specialist) reader.

Encyclopedia Talmudica: A digest of halachic literature and Jewish law from the Tannaitic period to the present time, under subject headings alphabetically arranged. Translated from the Hebrew and edited by *Prof. Isidore Epstein (obm)* and *Rabbi Dr Harry Freedman.*
Three volumes published to date.

Commentary on the Mishnah, by *Maimonides (Rambam)*
Introduction and Tractate Berachoth, translated into English by *Fred Rosner.* The first English rendition of this important classic. In the Introduction, a comprehensive work by itself, Maimonides deals with the Revelation at Sinai, transmission of the Oral Law down to Talmudic times, the nature of prophecy, and the types of law in the Mishnah. There follows an annotated translation of the commentary to *Berachoth,* the first part of Maimonides' work to make the Mishnah understandable to all.

שַׁעֲרֵי לִמּוּד

The Gateway to Learning

שַׁעֲרֵי לִמּוּד

The Gateway to Learning

*A systematic introduction
to the study of Talmud*

by

Eliyahu Krupnick

FELDHEIM PUBLISHERS

Jerusalem | New York

First published 1981
ISBN 0-87306-253-1

Phototypeset at the Feldheim Press

Philipp Feldheim Inc.
96 East Broadway
New York, NY 10002

Feldheim Publishers Ltd
POB 6525/Jerusalem, Israel

Printed in Israel

To

my beloved parents

Samson and Lillian Krupnick

untiring workers in the vineyard of *Hashem*

for a multitude of good causes

for the sake of

Torah, avodah and *gᵉmiluth chasadim*

over nearly half a century

with my heartfelt gratitude for the years of learning with which
they provided me, that preceded this book and made it
possible, and for their encouragement, guidance and assistance,
which has led to its publication. May they be blessed in all their
endeavors, and may Heaven grant them many more years, to
continue their splendid vital activity on behalf of the Torah
and those who learn it.

הרב חיים פינחס שינברג

ראש הישיבה „תורה אור"

מורה הוראה דקרית מטרסדורף

ירושלים — טלפון 521513

יום ד' לסדר אם בחקתי תלכו תש"מ

הנה הרב אליהו קרופניק נ"י, רחש לבו דבר טוב לזכות את הרבים בדבר נחוץ מאד, ספר הדרכה בדרכי למוד הגמרא ולקוט כללי הש"ס מספרי הראשונים והאחרונים פרי נסיונו כר"מ בישיבת איתרי חדרה. ובאשר אני מכיר את המחבר היטב ויודע שהצליח בע"ה להדריך תלמידים בדרך מישור בהבנת הגמרא, בטוחני שהספר **שערי למוד** יהי' לתועלת גדולה לתלמידי הישיבות ולמחנכים וכל מי שיחפש הדרך להבנת הגמרא.

והנני מברכו שיזכהו ה' לפתוח שערי הלמוד לפני העמלים בתורה כחפצו וכחפץ הכו"ח לכבוד התורה ולומדי'

חיים פינחס שיינברג

The greatest challenge facing the world of Torah education today is the development of a methodology to introduce the student with limited background in Jewish studies to the Talmud. We who have been granted the privilege of teaching Torah to a generation of young men with outstanding academic backgrounds from English-speaking countries are acutely aware of the problems they encounter in mastering the style and language of Talmudic studies.

It is therefore a great pleasure for us to welcome the publication of Rabbi Eliyahu Krupnick's excellent aid for this type of student. This concise work, representing a thorough research effort by a Talmudic scholar with years of teaching experience in Israel, will serve the novice in Talmud as a virtual tutor, helping him to navigate the Sea of Talmud with confidence and competence.

The points selected by the author for clarification demonstrate his sensitive appreciation of the obstacles encountered by students in their initial efforts towards gaining a mastery of the text. Such mastery is vital not only to the understanding of Talmud but to an intelligent approach towards the classic commentaries on Torah and the vast literature of Halacha. He is to be congratulated for the sophisticated manner in which he has restricted himself to the crucial problems facing the beginner so that the reader knows exactly what he can expect to find in this work as a guide to his development.

We recommend this work not only for students in Yeshivos such as ours but also for every student of Talmud who wishes to acquire a clearer understanding of the intricacies of the Talmud. May Heaven bless the author with the wide acceptance of his work and enable him to continue producing works to help Jews of all ages grow in their Torah development.

With Torah blessings,
RABBI MENDEL WEINBACH
Dean, Ohr Somayach Institutions

CONTENTS

A few notes on the transliteration and vocalization:

1) When a Hebrew term in transliteration is introduced, it appears in italics; thereafter, it appears in roman type, so as not to be distracting.

2) The small italic *e* (ᵉ) indicates the שְׁוָא נָע, pronounced like the second *e* in *peripheral*.

3) The *th* indicates ת, a letter pronounced like *t* in modern Israeli Hebrew and like *s* in Ashkenazic Hebrew, and pronounced as *th* by Yemenite Jews.

4) The Aramaic words in this book have been vocalized according to the rules of Aramaic grammar, and therefore are sometimes at variance with the pronunciation traditional in yeshivoth.

Introduction

אָמַר רַבִּי יוֹחָנָן: לֹא כָּרַת הַקָּדוֹשׁ־בָּרוּךְ־הוּא בְּרִית עִם יִשְׂרָאֵל אֶלָּא בִּשְׁבִיל דְּבָרִים שֶׁבְּעַל־פֶּה, שֶׁנֶּאֱמַר: כִּי עַל־פִּי הַדְּבָרִים הָאֵלֶּה כָּרַתִּי אִתְּךָ בְּרִית וְאֶת יִשְׂרָאֵל. (גיטין ס׳, ב) (Rabbi Yochanan stated, "The Holy One, Blessed be He, made His covenant with Israel only for the sake of the Oral Law.") The Written Law, i.e. the Bible, has become universally accepted. It is the Oral Law (תּוֹרָה שֶׁבְּעַל־פֶּה) that provides the exclusive guidance of the Jewish people, applying the general principles of the Written Law to the specific regulations and disciplines involved in a Torah way of life.

For example, the commandment וְהָיוּ לְטֹטָפֹת בֵּין עֵינֶיךָ (*and they shall be totaphoth between your eyes*) (דברים ו׳, ח) would have been completely incomprehensible without the clarification of תּוֹרָה שֶׁבְּעַל־פֶּה, which interpreted טֹטָפֹת as *t*e*fillin* (phylacteries) and described their preparation and use. Indeed, in one instance the Written Torah itself patently refers its readers to the Oral tradition: It commands וְזָבַחְתָּ . . . . כַּאֲשֶׁר צִוִּיתִךָ (*and you shall slaughter* [animals] . . . *in the manner which I have commanded you*) (דברים י״ב, כ״א) yet the exact details regarding slaughtering are not found anywhere in the Bible. Therefore, the Sages concluded that the Scripture refers to laws and instructions which God transmitted to Moshe on Mount Sinai (חולין כ״ח, א׳) .

Learning the תּוֹרָה שֶׁבְּעַל־פֶּה has always required much effort, time, and a total dedication to the study of its precepts; as the Midrash Tanchuma (נח, ג׳) says, תּוֹרָה שֶׁבְּעַל־פֶּה קָשָׁה לִלְמֹד וְיֵשׁ בָּהּ צַעַר גָּדוֹל שֶׁהִיא מְשׁוּלָה לַחֹשֶׁךְ (the Oral Law is difficult to learn and involves much anguish, for it is likened to darkness). And indeed, since the revelation of תּוֹרָה שֶׁבְּעַל־פֶּה at Sinai, the scholars throughout the generations have delved into its depths with total devotion, as the Midrash concludes, שֶׁאֵין לוֹמֵד אוֹתָהּ אֶלָּא מִי שֶׁאוֹהֵב הַקָּבָּ"ה בְּכָל לִבּוֹ וּבְכָל נַפְשׁוֹ (only he who loves the Holy One Blessed be He with all his heart and with all his soul can learn it).

In our times we have been fortunate to witness a remarkable return to tradition in general and to the study of תּוֹרָה שֶׁבְּעַל־פֶּה in particular. Regretfully, while many develop a strong desire to familiarize themselves with the Gᵉmara, they are disheartened by the difficulties involved in adjusting to the language and to the concepts of the Aramaic text. Even the many who continue to study Talmud for years in spite of the obstacles, do not always succeed in achieving a true understanding of Gᵉmara.

In my years of experience in teaching newcomers to yeshivoth I have found beyond dispute, that students with only a minimal background in Hebrew can become reasonably fluent in Gᵉmara reading and comprehension after only a few months of properly directed Gᵉmara study. Unfortunately, most beginners in the study of Gᵉmara lose a great deal of time simply developing the basic techniques of learning Talmud.

I have found that as a rule, a student of average intelligence can read and understand almost any Gᵉmara once he has mastered three fundamental skills. These include:

13
•

(1) certain basic background information about the way the Mishnah and G'mara were compiled and written;

(2) familiarity with the various structures of סֻגְיוֹת (Talmudic discussions);

(3) knowledge of the meaning and connotations of certain key words and expressions, as well as elementary grammar.

In this booklet we have בע"ה collected the necessary background information from the writings of the classic commentaries (רִאשׁוֹנִים וְאַחֲרוֹנִים); we have constructed a method of outlining סֻגְיוֹת, classifying them by their components; and finally, we have compiled a glossary of key words and expressions, giving the meanings and connotations of each. Hopefully, after mastering this material, the student need only learn through twenty or thirty pages of almost any G'mara, taking note (preferably in the form of a written outline) of the structure of each סֻגְיָא, and observing the basic words and expressions in action, in order to develop reasonable fluency in G'mara study within a few months. At that point, even if the student does not yet fully understand all the words in a סֻגְיָא he should nevertheless be able to grasp the meaning of the discussion in any G'mara on the basis of his acquired familiarity with the structure of the type of סֻגְיָא and the key words that signal the beginning of questions, answers, quotations, etc.

This suggested method for Talmud study should serve not only as an introduction to the reading and comprehension of G'mara, but should help to create a solid foundation for proper understanding of G'mara in depth at more advanced levels of learning. The method suggested in this booklet may also be used effectively by educators as a means of opening the

14
•

GATEWAY TO LEARNING

שַׁעֲרֵי לִמּוּד (the gateway to learning) to their students in an interesting way, with a minimum of effort.

In addition, we have appended a list of כְּלָלֵי הַשַּׁ"ס (rules and systems of the Talmud), compiled from many books of רִאשׁוֹנִים and אַחֲרוֹנִים, which are important at all levels of learning in order to facilitate the proper understanding of difficult procedures of the G'mara which give rise to problems of interpretation.

We wish the reader much success in the long, but rewarding, road to the understanding of תּוֹרָה שֶׁבְּעַל־פֶּה, and we hope fervently that this booklet will help him to become an additional link in the unbroken chain of teachers and disciples of תּוֹרָה שֶׁבְּעַל־פֶּה from Sinai to our day.

The תּוֹרָה שֶׁבְּעַל־פֶּה

background information

And I shall give you the tablets of stone and the Torah and the commandment:[1] "Torah" refers to the Written Torah; "the commandment" refers to its explanations,[2] the Oral Torah,[3] for all the commandments with all the details of their laws were given to Moshe on Mount Sinai.[4] This explanation of Torah was handed down orally with scrupulous care from one generation to another for thirty-five generations,[5] as in each generation tens of thousands of scholars delved into the study of every minute detail of תּוֹרָה שֶׁבְּעַל־פֶּה and the Sanhedrin (the supreme body of scholars) enacted regulations and restrictions when they deemed it necessary to preserve the sanctity of Torah laws.[6]

Then, after the destruction of the Second Temple, Rabbi Yehudah haNasi, whom Rambam described as a man of perfection in wisdom and piety,[7] wrote down the Oral Law for the first time, fearing that in the course of exile, persecution, and restrictions on learning, it was in danger of being forgotten.[8] He and many other Sages of his time carefully examined the various traditions and opinions transmitted over the years on all subjects within the תּוֹרָה שֶׁבְּעַל־פֶּה, and recorded them, using a minimum of carefully chosen words, thus compiling what became known as the Mishnah.[9]

In actuality, many of the laws of the Mishnah had already been arranged and summarized in Mishnah-like form before Rabbi Yehudah's time. They were memorized and handed down orally by scholars from one generation to another.[10] These *mishnayoth* (teachings or sections of such Oral Law) were grouped together because of certain similarities that facilitated memorization, and not necessarily on the basis of subject division. Rabbi Yehudah, even after re-organizing the *mishnayoth* on the basis of subject, occasionally retained the old structure, since the *mishnayoth* had already been accepted and memorized by the people at large in this form. It was of utmost importance to him to avoid the confusion which might result from change, thus disrupting memorization. This is why we find *mishnayoth* which include subjects not directly connected to their tractate.[11]

In the same manner, we sometimes find two statements in a *mishnah*, of which the second is more inclusive than the first, making the first apparently unnecessary. This phenomenon is referred to by the G‘mara (authoritative body of explanation and interpretation of the Mishnah; see below) as לֹא זוּ אַף זוּ. On other occasions, the first is more inclusive than the second; this is termed זוּ וְאֵין צָרִיךְ לוֹמַר זוּ. These types of statements originated when Rabbi Yehudah first learned the simpler statement from his teachers and incorporated it in his Mishnah. Only after it had become well-known and memorized did he hear the more inclusive ruling, and rather than eliminate the already accepted statement, he simply added the additional information.[12]

There are cases where the Mishnah follows the opinion of a certain Tanna (scholar of the Mishnaic period) in one place, while following a conflicting opinion in another! This occurred because Rabbi Yehudah initially felt the first Tanna's opinion to be the correct one. Years later, when he added the conflicting *mishnah*, he had changed his opinion about the correct decision of the *halachah*; nevertheless, he did not eliminate the original *mishnah*, since it had already been memorized by the learned people, and change would create confusion.[13] This concern for clarity in order to facilitate memorization led Rabbi Yehudah to maintain similarity and symmetry between the language and the subject matter of adjacent statements in the Mishnah.[14]

The Mishnah was written in a terse style on the assumption that the scholars of each generation would fully grasp all the implications, transmitting them accordingly. It is for this reason that the G'mara often explains passages of the Mishnah in a way that differs from their apparent meaning (הָכִי קָאֲמַר), or refers a passage to some specific situation though the Mishnah does not specify one (הָכָא בְּמַאי עָסְקִינָן).[15] A passage is sometimes interpreted as if seemingly missing words had been inserted (חַסּוֹרֵי מְחַסְּרָא); this does not intend to correct the Mishnah, but simply to note the words that Rabbi Yehudah relied upon the reader to understand as if they were written.[16]

However, on account of the declining level of scholarship that Rabbi Yehudah had foreseen, his disciples found it necessary to write down explanations of the Mishnah only a short time after its compilation. This task was accomplished by Rabbi Chiyya[17] in his compilation of teachings that had been quoted by Tannaim in Rabbi Yehudah's presence and with his agreement. This is called *tosefta* (addition to the Mishnah).[18] At about the same time, the *b'raithoth* (literally,

externals) were compiled by Rabbi Chiyya, Rabbi Oshaya, and
Bar Kappara.[19] They are a collection of Tannaitic statements
which are neither direct explanations of the Mishnah, nor
were they stated in Rabbi Yehudah's presence; they are,
rather, statements made outside of his *beth midrash*
(academy).[20] These include Rav's compilations of laws derived
from the verses in *Vayikra* (Leviticus): תּוֹרַת כּוֹהֲנִים or סְפְרָא דְּבֵי
רַב; and in *Bᵉmidbar* (Numbers) and *Dᵉvarim* (Deuteronomy):
שְׁאָר סִפְרֵי דְּבֵי רַב or סִפְרֵי in short.[21] Since there were other
compilations of *bᵉraithoth* and later compilations of the *tosefta*
which were less reliable, the Gᵉmara occasionally refuses to
accept a proof from these sources on the grounds that it is in
error (מְשַׁבֶּשְׁתָּא), coming from an unreliable source.[22] We can
thus understand the reasoning behind a passage in the Gᵉmara
which first explains the difficulties of a particular *baraitha*
(generally pronounced *bᵉraitha*) before using it to prove a
point: it does so in order to assure first that it is not מְשַׁבֶּשְׁתָּא.[23]

With the end of the period of the Tannaim there began a
three-hundred-year period[24] (seven generations)[25] of the
Amoraim (literally, explainers).[26] Realizing that they were no
longer on a level of scholarship that would permit them to
disagree with the Tannaim,[27] they devoted all their efforts to
understanding, clarifying, and elucidating the teachings of
these predecessors, primarily as expressed in the Mishnah.[28]

When the Sages again noted that the level of scholarship
was diminishing, and further dispersion in exile was
imminent, they decided to commit to writing the conclusions
of the halachic discussion in the various yeshivoth over the
centuries. The Jerusalem Talmud was thus compiled by Rabbi
Yochanan,[29] one of Rabbi Yehudah's younger disciples, who
subsequently become the leading scholar in the Land of Israel.

The Babylonian Talmud (G‘mara) was compiled by Ravina and Rav Ashi, who spent sixty years collecting, examining, and organizing all that had been stated before them. It was later completed by Merémar and Mar, the son of Rav Ashi, in the year 4265 (505 C.E.) with some additions by the Sages who followed them, the Savoraim.[30]

The Amoraim had four purposes in writing the G‘mara: 1. to explain the reasoning behind the laws of the Mishnah; 2. to render a final ruling of *halachah* on differences of opinion between Tannaim and between Amoraim; 3. to record the rabbinical decrees and enactments made after the Mishnaic period; 4. to collect the דְּרָשׁוֹת וְאַגָּדוֹת (homiletic literature)[31] which allude to all the concepts of philosophy[32] and the hidden teachings of the Kabbalah.[33] (Rambam and leading Kabbalists all point out that the Talmud doesn't just relate to, but solves all the problems of philosophy and hints at all the hidden teachings of Kabbalah to those who are capable of this understanding.)

The G‘mara is a record of discussions held in yeshivoth at various times and places, noting not only conclusions but also the thought processes which led to them.[34] This is why we occasionally find a question asked concerning an Amora's statement which could have logically been asked about a statement made earlier on the page, simply because that was the way the discussion happened to develop![35] Similarly, sometimes two overlapping halachic questions are recorded in the G‘mara, because each was asked in a different yeshivah, unknown to one another.[36] Unlike Tannaim, Amoraim expressed their meanings much more clearly; therefore, the

G'mara does not attempt to explain their sayings with anything other than their literal meanings.[37]

Thus, out of countless utterances of hundreds of thousands of scholars over a period of forty generations, Rabbi Yehudah, Ravina, Rav Ashi and the scholars of their generations carefully chose the most reliable statements of only a few of the greatest Tannaim and Amoraim, and thus summarized the תּוֹרָה שֶׁבְּעַל־פֶּה for all future generations.[38] Since the G'mara was completed, the scholars of subsequent generations would not disagree with Amoraim or derive new laws from the Written Torah; instead, they concentrated upon a comprehensive understanding of the Oral Law, solving all halachic problems by analysis of and comparison with Talmudic sources.[39]

The תּוֹרָה שֶׁבְּעַל־פֶּה as presented in the Talmud (Mishnah and G'mara) may be divided into five parts:[40]

1. Laws handed down by Moshe Rabbeinu to which there is reference in Scripture; for example, פְּרִי עֵץ הָדָר (the fruit of a beautiful tree)[41] refers to the ethrog, which each generation has used through the line of tradition going back to Moshe and Yehoshua in observance of the mitzvah; yet, the Sages also found a reference or allusion to it in the Written Torah.[42]

2. Laws handed down by Moshe Rabbeinu for which no source or reference can be found in the Written Torah — הֲלָכָה לְמשֶׁה מִסִּינַי.

3. Laws derived by the מִדּוֹת שֶׁהַתּוֹרָה נִדְרֶשֶׁת בָּהֶן (methods by which the Torah may be expounded). Most of the מַחֲלוֹקוֹת (halachic differences) developed within this category, primarily from the time that disciples of Hillel and Shammai (about one hundred years before the destruction of the Second Temple) no longer fully mastered the application of these

methods of derivation with the same perfection as their predecessors.[43]

4. Rabbinical prohibitions made in order to prevent transgression of Torah laws, as the Torah commands, וּשְׁמַרְתֶּם אֶת מִשְׁמַרְתִּי (And you shall guard My treasured laws),[44] which the G'mara interpreted to mean, עֲשׂוּ מִשְׁמֶרֶת לְמִשְׁמַרְתִּי (make a protection for My treasured laws).[45] Here too, we find differences of opinion among the Tannaim and Amoraim as to whether a particular prohibition is necessary or desirable.

5. Other ordinances, customs, and measures concerning the public welfare which the scholars found necessary to enact and establish.

מאימתי

מזכירין גבורות גשמים רבי אליעזר אומר
מיום טוב הראשון של חג ר' יהושע אומר
מיום טוב האחרון של חג אמר ליה לר' יהושע
הואיל ואין הגשמים סימן קללה בחג
למה הוא מזכיר אמר לו אף אני
לא אמרתי לשאול אלא להזכיר משיב הרוח
ומוריד הגשם בעונתו אמר לו א"כ לעולם
יהא מזכיר אין שואלין את הגשמים אלא
סמוך לגשמים ר' יהודה אומר העובר לפני
התיבה ביום טוב האחרון של חג הארון מזכיר
הראשון אינו מזכיר ביום טוב הראשון של פסח
הראשון מזכיר האחרון אינו מזכיר גמ' תנא
היכא קאי דקתני מאימתין תנא התם
קאי דקתני מזכירין גבורות גשמים בתחיה
הרוח ישראלין בברכת השנים ותקעו גבורה
בדינון דקתני וקרנו מאימתי מזכירין גבורות
גשמים וליהדר היכא קאי גמ' דעבדקיה עד ובא

ולירחני מזכירין מאי הכא התם תנא והרגא ובת נידונין
גשמים וליהנדני מאימתי מזכירין על הגשמים
מאי דקתני גשמים אד תרתין מפני שיורד
גשם ובנגבורה שנאמר "עושה גדולות עד אין
חקר ונפלאות עד אין מספר וכתיב הרונתן
מטר על פני ארץ ושלח מים על פני חוצות
כתיב מישתם אדם של עולם הא כתיב בא עושה
חקך גבורות של עולם אין חקר וכתוב הרם "ולא
אלא אי שמעת אלה עולם היל בא מהן קצות
הארץ יעפל לא יינע ואין חקר לתבונתו ומכא
"וכתיב מכין הרם בכרד נאזר בגבורה וכתיב
ל דבתפלה רתניא "לאהבה את ד' אלהיכם
ולעבדו בכל לבבבכם איזו היא עבודה שהיא
בלב הוי אומר זו תפלה וכתיב בתריה "ונתתי מטר ארצכם בעתו יורה
ומלקוש אמר ר' יוחנן 'ג' מפתחות בידו של הקב"ה שלא נמסרו ביד שליח
ואלו הן מפתח של (א) גשמים ומפתח של חיה ומפתח של תחיית המתים
מטר ארצך בעתו דכתיב "יפתח ד' לך את אוצרו הטוב בו ד' ארצך בעתו וישמע
אליה

The components of a page of Talmud

A מִשְׁנָה

a paragraph of the Mishnah.

B גְּמָרָא

the G⁽ᵉ⁾mara, which explains, elucidates and discusses the Mishnah.

C רַשִׁ"י

the basic, essential commentary on the Talmud, known by the name of its author, Rashi (an abbreviation of Rabbeinu Sh⁽ᵉ⁾lomo Yitzchaki, i.e. R. Sh⁽ᵉ⁾lomo ben Yitzchak), a famed 11th-century scholar of Troyes, France. Unsurpassed in its elucidation and interpretation of the Talmudic text, it has remained an integral part of Talmud study ever since its appearance.

D תּוֹסָפוֹת

Tos⁽ᵃ⁾foth: a series of commentaries on the tractates of the Talmud by scholars of France and Germany in the 11th to 13th centuries, which generally compare or contrast a סָגְיָא of the Talmud with related סָגְיוֹת found elsewhere in the Talmud.

E עֵין מִשְׁפָּט

Ein Mishpat: references indicating where in the *Shulchan Aruch* and other codes of Jewish law a passage of the Talmud is the basis of a *halachah*.

F הַגָּהוֹת הַבַּ"ח

Hagahoth haBach: corrections of printers' errors and occasional notes on the Talmud by R. Yoel Sirkes, of 18th-century Poland. The name Bach, as he was generally known, is an abbreviation of the title of his work בַּיִת חָדָשׁ, which brought him renown.

G מְסוֹרֶת הַשַּׁ"ס

M⁽ᵉ⁾soreth ha-Shass: cross-references to identical or similar passages elsewhere in the G⁽ᵉ⁾mara.

סֻגְיָא
structures

All סֻגְיוֹת of the Talmud may be subdivided into nine components.[46] These are:

1. פֵּרוּשׁ (explanation of the mishnah)

2. שְׁאֵלָה וּתְשׁוּבָה (halachic question and answer)

3. קֻשְׁיָא וּפֵרוּק (question raised to refute a Talmudic statement, and its resolution)

4. סִיּוּעַ (support and proof of a Talmudic statement)

5. רְמִיָּה (the pointing out of apparent contradictions between Tannaitic or Biblical statements)

6. הַצְרָכָה (explaining the need for two apparently similar statements by pointing out unique elements in each one)

7. הִלְכְתָא (halachic ruling)

8. מַעֲשֶׂה (an account of a ruling rendered in an actual case to support a halachic opinion)

9. אַגָּדָה or הַגָּדָה (homiletic teaching and narrative)

25
•
SUGYA STRUCTURES

We may identify and analyze these components as follows:

1. פֵּרוּשׁ — Explanations of the mishnah are usually introduced by the question: ... מַאי (What is the meaning of ...)[47]

2. שְׁאֵלָה וּתְשׁוּבָה — The question is generally introduced by the words בַּעְיָא לְהוּ (they asked of them) when a group of scholars asked the question of another group of scholars or of themselves; it begins בְּעוֹ מִנֵּהּ (they asked of him) when a group asks an individual; or, בָּעָא מִנֵּהּ (he asked of him) when one individual asks another.[48] Sometimes the Gᵉmara provides no answer, leaving the question with the comment תֵּיקוּ (let it stand, i.e. let it remain unanswered). (ועי׳ שו״ת חת״ס חו״מ, לקוטים צ״ח)

3. קֻשְׁיָא וּפֵרוּק — If the question stems from a quotation of a Tannaitic source (mishnah, baraitha, or tosefta) it is usually introduced with the word מֵיתִיבִי (they asked), or, if asked by an individual, אֵיתֵבֵהּ (he asked him).[49] If a question of logic is raised by an Amora, it is introduced with the expression מַתְקֵף לַהּ,[50] or פָּרֵךְ or מְגַדֵּף; some say that the latter two are questions injected by the Savoraim after the Amoraic period.[51]

When an Amora is confronted with a Tannaitic statement that seems to contradict his opinion, he will generally retort in one of three ways: (a) by interpreting the Tanna's statement in such a way that it no longer contradicts him; (b) by stating that the mishnah, tosefta, or baraitha follows the opinion of a certain Tanna, whereas he, the Amora, follows a conflicting Tannaitic opinion — this type of answer is introduced by the words מַנִּי, רַבִּי פְּלוֹנִי הִיא (the source of this statement is Rabbi ...);[52] (c) by proclaiming the baraitha mistaken, stemming from an unreliable source (מְשַׁבְּשָׁתָא).[53]

If the Amora finds no way to reconcile his view with the

Tannaitic source or to answer the logical objection to his statement, the Gᵉmara will usually conclude that the question is a תְּיוּבְתָּא (refutation) of the Amora's opinion, or will sometimes conclude that it is merely קַשְׁיָא (difficult), implying that the opinion has not been totally refuted by the question.[54]

4. סִיוּעַ—A statement of this type will be introduced by לֵימָא מְסַיַּע לֵהּ (may we say that this supports his opinion).

5. רְמִיָּה—A statement of this type will be introduced by וּרְמִינְהִי (literally, we cast one against the other). When the contradiction is between two statements within the same mishnah, the expression used is קַשְׁיָא רֵישָׁא אַסֵּיפָא (the first statement contradicts the latter).

6. הַצְרָכָה—This is introduced by the word צְרִיכִי (they are necessary).[55]

7. הִלְכְתָא—It is usually introduced by וְהִלְכְתָא . . . (and the halachic ruling is . . .).

8. מַעֲשֶׂה—This is often introduced in Tannaitic sources by the word מַעֲשֶׂה . . . (an actual case occurred . . .) and in the Gᵉmara by . . . הֲוָה עֻבְדָּא (meaning the same).[56]

9. אַגָּדָה—This kind of statement has no fixed introductory expression, but often begins with a quotation of a Biblical verse, followed by interpretation and elucidation.

Examples of the components within a סֻגְיָא and the interplay between them, together with instructions on how to outline a סֻגְיָא, will be demonstrated in Section Four, entitled "Exercise in סֻגְיָא Analysis."

TABLE OF COMPONENTS

Component	Purpose	Key term
פֵּרוּשׁ	Explanation of a passage of Mishnah	מַאי
שְׁאֵלָה וּתְשׁוּבָה	Resolution of a halachic question	אִבַּעְיָא לְהוּ / בְּעוֹ מִנֵּהּ / בְּעָא מִנֵּהּ
קַשְׁיָא וּפֵרוּק	Resolution of a difficulty in a Talmudic statement	מֵיתִיבִי / אֵיתֵבֵהּ / מַתְקֵף לַהּ / פָּרֵךְ / מְגַדֵּף
סִיּוּעַ	Support for a Talmudic statement	לֵימָא מְסַיַּע לֵהּ
רְמִיָּה	Resolution of a contradiction between Talmudic or Biblical statements	וּרְמִינְהִי
הַצְרָכָה	Explanation of the need for a similar (apparently superfluous) statement	צְרִיכִי
הִלְכְתָא	Halachic ruling	וְהִלְכְתָא
מַעֲשֶׂה	Illustration of a halachic ruling in an actual case	מַעֲשֶׂה הַנָּה עָבְדָּא
אַגָּדָה	Homiletic (or ethical) teaching, or narrative	

Key words and expressions*

אִי אָמְרַתְּ בִּשְׁלָמָא "if you said ... it would be acceptable": implying that since you have said otherwise, the following objection may be raised.

אִי הָכִי "if so": introduces an apparent difficulty in the statement of a colleague; according to the scholar's own opinion, however, there exists no such difficulty.

אִינִי ... וְהָא (literally: can that be) "it is not so, for ... ": this is an introduction to a question, implying that it could not be so, for Rabbi ... said, etc.

אֶלָּא "but rather": often used after a previous answer has been disproved, as an introduction to an alternative answer.

אֶלָּא וַדַּאי "but certainly": used when the alternative answer is proved to be conclusively correct. (דרכי הגמרא)

אַלְמָא "hence; consequently; so we see (from this)": usually followed by a question on what has been deduced. (יד מלאכי פ' בשם ש"מ ב"ק ק צ"ט ב)

---

*Based on definitions in הליכות עולם, שער ב; other sources are noted individually.

אַלָּמָא (אַלָּמָה) "why . . . ?"

אִלְמָלֵא (אִלְמָלֵי) "if it were not that; if not for; but for" (see תוס׳ מגילה כ״א א, ד״ה אלמלא).

אִלְמָלֵי (אִלְמָלֵא) "if; if indeed" (see *ibid.* תוס׳ שם); this and the preceding term are at times spelled interchangeably.

. . . אָמַר רַבִּי . . . אָמַר רַבִּי "Rabbi . . . related that Rabbi . . . had said": a statement heard directly from the original source. (כריתות ה׳, ג׳; יד מלאכי ע״ה, קיצור כללי התלמוד)

. . . אָמַר רַבִּי . . . מִשּׁוּם רַבִּי "Rabbi . . . said in the name of Rabbi . . .": an indirect quotation, not heard directly from the original source. (כריתות ה׳, ג׳) Some hold that this form indicates that the Tanna or Amora speaking does not agree with the statement he quotes. (יד מלאכי ע״ה, קיצור כללי התלמוד)

אַסְמַכְתָּא a Scriptural text cited to support a Rabbinical enactment; some hold that the Torah thus hinted the precept to the Sages and left it to their discretion whether to make it mandatory (ריטב״א ר״ה ט״ז א; מהר״ל, באר הגולה, באר א׳; ועי׳ רמב״ם, הקדמה לפירוש המשנה); others hold that the Sages received the inspiration to enact their law from the concept taught in the Scriptural text (של״ה, כלל רבנן). Occasionally an אַסְמַכְתָּא is found for a הֲלָכָה לְמשֶׁה מִסִּינַי (ש״י בשם רמב״ן).

אִתְּמַר (אִתַּמַר) "it has been said": introduction to a statement of an Amora (see מֵימְרָא).

בְּדִיעֲבַד "if it has already been done (improperly)"; short for דְּאִי עֲבַד.

קָמִפְּלְגִי (בְּמַאי קָמִפַּלְגִי) "what is the matter at issue?"; what are the reasons behind the two opinions?

גּוּפָא "the matter itself": introduces an in-depth discussion of a text or subject that was touched upon previously in passing; it indicates that previously the statement was brought casually, but now it has become the focus of the discussion itself. The expression אָמַר מַר "the master (previously) stated," also refers back to a previously mentioned statement, but is used even when the statement was the major subject under discussion.

גְּמִירִי (הִלְכְתָא גְּמִירִי) "we have learned": referring to traditions which, as a rule, were transmitted orally by Moshe from Sinai (see Part 1).

דַּיְקָא נַמִּי "you may also deduce it": this expression and הָכִי נַמִּי מִסְתַּבְּרָא "so it also follows by reasoning" introduce a proof for the validity of an answer or an interpretation. The difference between the two is that דַּיְקָא נַמִּי introduces a deduction from the wording of the very text under discussion, whereas הָכִי נַמִּי מִסְתַּבְּרָא introduces a proof from an external source or reasoning. (דרכי הגמרא; ועי״ יד מלאכי רכ״ד)

הָא גּוּפָא קַשְׁיָא "this is self-contradictory" (דרכי הגמרא)

הַאי מַאי?! "what is this?!": an exclamation of dismay at a comparison of two totally different matters. (דרכי הגמרא)

הַוֵּי, הַוֵּינַן "he examined, we examined": introduction to Talmudic questioning and examination of a mishnah.

הֵיכִי דָמִי "what is the case?": introduces a question as to what type of situation a general statement is referring to. (דרכי הגמרא)

הֵיכִי מְשַׁכַּחַת לַהּ "how may it be found?": asked when a practical application of a statement or principle seems impossible or difficult to envision. (דרכי הגמרא)

וְאָמְרִי לָהּ "and some say it"—some say that Rabbi . . . made the aforementioned statement and not Rabbi . . . who had been incorrectly quoted.

וּדְקָ(א)רֵי לֵהּ מַאי קָ(א)רֵי לֵהּ "and when he compared it how did he come to compare it?": asked occasionally when a refutation of a statement appears so obvious that the G'mara wonders what the Amora had in mind when he made his statement. (According to הליכות עולם, this (מהרי"ק ב' א' בשם הערוך; ועי' יד מלאכי קל"ח) type of question was introduced by the Savoraim.) Similarly, the expression מִידִי אָרְיָא means "are they really comparable?" (מהרי"ק, שם)

וְהָא תְּנַן, וְהָא תַּנְיָא "and we have learned": introduction to a quotation of a Tannaitic statement that supports what has been said. (רש"י פ"ק דב"ק)

וְהָתְנַן, וְהָתַנְיָא "but we have learned": introduction to a quotation of a Tannaitic statement which contradicts what has been said. Occasionally the terms appear as וְהָא תְּנַן, וְהָא תַּנְיָא.

כְּגוֹן זֶה "all things similar to this": implies that even things which are only partially similar may be deduced from this precedent. (כנה"ג, קס"ה)

כִּי אֲתָא "when he came"—from Eretz Yisrael to Babylonia (the two centers of Torah learning from the time of the destruction of the First Temple until the completion of the Jerusalem and Babylonian Talmuds). (הקדמת הסמ"ג)

כִּי סָלֵק "when he went up" from Babylon to Eretz Yisrael.

לָא צְרִיכָא "it is not necessary" (short for לָא צְרִיכָא אֶלָּא): the Sage's statement is necessary only for the following case.

לְהוֹדִיעֲךָ כֹּחוֹ דְּרַבִּי ... "to tell you the authority of Rabbi ... ": to emphasize the strength and extent of his halachic ruling.

לֵימָא, נֵימָא "shall we say"—introduces a possible deduction which is usually disproved in the conclusion.(כללי מהרי״ק ז׳, ב)

לֵימָא הָנֵי תַּנָּאֵי כְּהָנֵי תַּנָּאֵי "shall we say that these Tannaim argue about the same point as did the other Tannaim?" When this is asked regarding statements found in the Mishnah, the G'mara inquires, "If both arguments are identical, why were they quoted in different mishnayoth rather than being placed together in one mishnah?" When it is asked regarding statements made in a baraitha, the G'mara wants to verify whether the arguments are identical, in order to arrive at a proper and correct ruling.

לֵימָא כְּתַנָּאֵי "shall we say that Tannaim have already argued on the subject of this Amoraic statement?" What concerns the G'mara is why the Amora made an apparently independent statement instead of formulating his statement as a ruling according to one of the Tannaim.

מַאי בֵּינַיְהוּ "what is the difference between them?" This is usually asked when two explanations are given for a law, and the G'mara seeks a halachic difference between the two explanations. It is also occasionally used in the sense of "What is the rationale behind the two opinions?" when the halachic difference is known, but not the reason behind it.

מַאי הֲוֵי עֲלַהּ "what is the conclusion about it?": a request for a final conclusion and halachic decision on a question which has so far been discussed inconclusively.

מַאי לָאו "is it not ... ?" This should be read as a question and tentative answer: מַאי "What (is it referring to)?" לָאו "Is it not . . . ?" (דרכי הגמרא)

מַאי קָא מַשְׁמַע לָן, תְּנֵינָא "What has he conveyed to us? (What new point has he taught us that we did not know previously?) We have learned that . . . " This is asked when an Amora makes a statement that is already well known from a mishnah (but not from a baraitha, which was generally not so well known). מַאי קָא מַשְׁמַע לָן is also asked occasionally when the statement was previously made by an Amora whose words are common knowledge.

מַאי קְרָאָה "what verse in the Torah (is it based on)?" This is asked when no explicit source in the Torah is known.

מַאן חֲכָמִים רַבִּי . . . "who are the Sages (referred to in a mishnah or a baraitha)?—Rabbi . . . " The Gᵉmara thus attempts to trace a majority opinion held by many scholars to its original source, which was one Sage's statement.
(רמב״ם, הקדמה לפירוש המשנה)

מַהוּ דְתֵימָא "you might have thought": introduction to an incorrect statement; if not for what had been said, you might have mistakenly thought that, etc. This statement is usually followed by קָא מַשְׁמַע לָן "therefore he informed us that," etc.

מַה נַּפְשָׁךְ, מִמַּה נַּפְשָׁךְ "whichever you choose"—introduction to a set of questions showing that whichever of the two possibilities is chosen, there will still remain a difficulty. (דרכי הגמרא)

מֵימְרָא "statement"—of an Amora, in the name of other Amoraim.

מְנָא לָן, מְנָא הָנֵי מִלֵּי "what is the source of this? from where are these words derived?"—asked in reference to subjects which have a source in the Torah.

מַעַרְבָא "the west": used in reference to Eretz Yisrael which is located southwest of Babylonia. (קצור כללי התלמוד)

מִשּׁוּם שֶׁנֶּאֱמַר "because it is stated, on account of the statement" (in the Torah), which provides an אַסְמַכְתָּא for a law.

סַבְרוּהַ "the scholars thought": usually introduces a supposition which is ultimately disproved. Occasionally however, the supposition remains valid even in the conclusion.
(כריתות שער ג׳ כלל ג׳)

. . . סְתָמָא דְּלָא כְּרַבִּי "this unchallenged statement in the mishnah is not according to Rabbi . . ." The Gᶜmara is disturbed by the fact that Rabbi Yehudah haNasi cited an individual's opinion in the mishnah as though there had been no disagreement about it, while there were, in actuality, Tannaim who disagreed.

קָא סָלְקָא דַּעְתֵּהּ "he thought": an elucidation of the reasoning of an Amora whose question was subsequently answered.

רַבָּנָן בֵּי רַב "the students in the beth midrash," not necessarily of the Amora named Rav. (רש״י קידושין מ״ז ב)

שְׁמַעְתְּתָא "statement, portion of Gᶜmara," referring to statements of Amoraim.

שֶׁנֶּאֱמַר "as it is stated" (in the Torah), giving the source of a law.

תָּא שְׁמַע "come and hear": introduction to a question or support based on a proof usually from a Tannaitic source, but occasionally from Scripture or logic. (כנה״ג קל״א, קל״ב)

35

KEY WORDS & EXPRESSIONS

תֶּהֱוֵי בָּהּ רַבִּי ... "Rabbi ... queried concerning it": a Rabbi examined the statement of an Amora to find the reasoning behind it.

תְּיוּבְתָּא דְּרַבִּי "a refutation of Rabbi ..." When this is the entire phrase, it indicates a question to the students (scholars) in the beth midrash: "Shall we say that this is a refutation of Rabbi ... ?" If the phrase is תְּיוּבְתָּא דְּרַבִּי ... תְּיוּבְתָּא, the second תְּיוּבְתָּא signifies that the students arrived at a consensus that the opinion was refuted. (כריתות בל״ל ש״ג, ת״ח ש״ג, פ״א ס״ט)

תְּנָא "it was learned"—in a tosefta. (כריתות ה׳ ג׳)

תַּנָּא תּוּנָא "the Tanna of our mishnah supports my opinion" (רש״י ב״מ ג׳ א)

תְּנוּ רַבָּנָן "the rabbis learned"—introduction to a known baraitha. (קיצור כללי התלמוד, בשם רש״י תענית י״א א ב; ועי׳ כריתות שער ה׳ כלל א׳, שכל "תנו רבנן" מקורו בספרא)

תְּנֵי חֲדָא, תַּנְיָא אִידָּךְ "it was learned in one (baraitha), it was learned in another (baraitha)"—introduces a baraitha which is not so well known. (מבוא התלמוד)

תְּנֵינָא לְהָא דְּתָנוּ רַבָּנָן "we have learned in the mishnah what was stated in the following baraitha"—proving that the baraitha is correct and the halachah may be set according to it.

תְּנֵי עֲלַהּ "it was learned (in a tosefta) in connection with it (a mishnah)": introduces an explanation of a mishnaic passage, given by a tosefta. (מבוא התלמוד)

תְּנֵי תַּנָּא קַמֵּהּ דְּרַב ... "an Amora quoted the following baraitha in the presence of Rabbi ..." (who had not known this particular baraitha).

תְּנַן "we have learned": introduction to a quotation from a mishnah, and occasionally from a baraitha.

(כנה"ג קנ"ז מבנימין זאב שכ"ב)

תְּנַן הָתָם "we have learned there": introduces a mishnah quoted from a different tractate.

תִּסְתַּיֵּם "it may be concluded that . . . ": introduces a proof based on a logical deduction, usually identifying the Sage who taught a particular statement or ruling. When it appears only once, it denotes a question (may it be concluded that . . . ?); when repeated, it is to be read as a statement of certainty — as with תְּיַבְתָּא.

. . . תִּפֹּק לֵהּ מִ "derive it (let it be derived) from . . . " — meaning, "Why is this derivation not enough?" The question is either (a) Why didn't you give a simpler derivation, (b) Why did you need so many derivations or sources, or (c) Why did you permit it? Is this derivation (basis) not enough to prohibit it?

תִּפְשֹׁט מֶהָא "solve your question from this": used when a solution is about to be found in a baraitha.

תִּפְשֹׁט מֶהָכָא "solve your question from here": used when the proof is found in an Amoraic statement.

תַּרְתֵּי "two" — conflicting or repetitious statements. (כריתות ה' ג')

Other key words which appear in the Talmud should be jotted down and memorized in order to avoid unnecessary repetition of mistakes and misunderstandings.

Tannaim always spoke in Hebrew, except for the language of legal documents and rabbinical decrees. קיצור כללי; (כריתות ה' ב')

(התלמוד בשם תוס', פרק אין מעמידים)

Tannaim were given the title רַבִּי or רַבָּן. The greatest among them were given no title at all, such as הִלֵּל and שַׁמַּאי (רמב״ם, הקדמה לפירוש המשנה). An Amora in Eretz Yisrael who received סְמִיכָה (ordination) was also called רַבִּי, while an Amora in Babylonia, where סְמִיכָה could not be given, was called רַב.

A list of leading Tannaim and Amoraim of each generation of the Mishnah and Gᵉmara periods may be found in הליכות עולם (שער א׳ פרק ב׳). Clarification of unclear and ambiguous names and surnames may be found there in שער א׳ פרק ג׳ or in Rambam's introduction to his commentary on the Mishnah.

QUESTIONS AND ANSWERS

Difficulty	Resolution	Concluding term when solution not found
שְׁאֵלָה *(halachic question)*	(1) answer based on logic (2) answer based on a Tannaitic source	תֵּיקוּ *(the question is left unresolved)*
קַשְׁיָא *(attack on an Amora's statement)*		
a. based on logic	logical answer	תְּיֻבְתָּא / קַשְׁיָא
b. based on a Tannaitic source	(1) alternate interpretation of source (2) conclusion that the source follows one Tanna, and the Amora another (3) the source is declared מְשַׁבֶּשְׁתָּא (uncertain, of doubtful accuracy)	תְּיֻבְתָּא קַשְׁיָא
רְמִיָּה *(contradiction)*	(1) interpretation which resolves the contradiction (2) explanation that each refers to a different situation	conclusion that they follow opinions of conflicting Tannaim
הַצְרָכָה *(why repetition by a similar, apparently superfluous statement)*	demonstration of a unique (separate) need for each statement	

Common Grammatical Prefixes and Suffixes

	Past	Present	Future	Possessive	
I (אֲנִי)	—	־ֵאנִי	אֶ־	my	־ִי , ־ַי
you (ms) (אַתָּה)	—	־ֶה	־ִתּ	your	־ְךָ , ־ֶיךָ
you (fs) (אַתְּ)	—	־ֶת	תִּ־ִי	his	־ֹה , ־ָיו
he (הוּא)	—	־וֹא	יִ־	her	־ָה , ־ֶיהָ
she (הִיא)	—	־ֶאנָה	תִּ־	our	־ֵנוּ , ־ֵינוּ
we (אֲנַחְנוּ)	—	־ִים	־ִי	your	־ְכֶם , ־ֵיכֶם
you (mp) (אַתֶּם)	—	־ִים	תִּ־וּ	their	־ֶהם , ־ֵיהֶם
you (fp) (אַתֶּן, אַתֵּנָה)	—	־וֹת	תִּ־נָה		
they (m) (הֵם, הֵמָּה)	—	־ִים	יִ־וּ		
they (f) (הֵן, הֵנָּה)	—	־וֹת	תִּ־נָה		

The letter א at the beginning of a word often takes the place of the Hebrew word עַל: for example, אַאֲרְצָא means "on the ground."

4

Exercise in סֻגְיָא analysis

Now, with the background information in mind, we are ready to examine the components, structure, and language of a סֻגְיָא. The following is a typical סֻגְיָא, which we will attempt to put into outline form and divide according to its components and key words.

(ברכות כ״ו א)

מִשְׁנָה: תְּפִלַּת הַשַּׁחַר עַד חֲצוֹת. רַבִּי יְהוּדָה אוֹמֵר: עַד ד' שָׁעוֹת. תְּפִלַּת הַמִּנְחָה עַד הָעֶרֶב. רַבִּי יְהוּדָה אוֹמֵר: עַד פְּלַג הַמִּנְחָה. תְּפִלַּת הָעֶרֶב אֵין לָהּ קֶבַע; וְשֶׁל מוּסָפִין — כָּל הַיּוֹם. רַבִּי יְהוּדָה אוֹמֵר: עַד ז' שָׁעוֹת.

גְּמָרָא: וּרְמִינְהִי: מִצְוָתָהּ עִם הָנֵץ

MISHNAH The morning t'fillah* [may be recited] until midday. Rabbi Yehudah says: until the fourth hour. The afternoon t'fillah [may be recited] till evening. Rabbi Yehudah says: until the middle of the afternoon. The evening prayer has no fixed limit. The time for the additional prayers is the whole of the day. Rabbi Yehudah says: till the seventh hour.

GEMARA ["Until midday":] This was contrasted with the following: The

*This denotes the *Amidah* or Sh'moneh Esréh.

הַחַמָּה, כְּדֵי שֶׁיִּסְמֹךְ גְּאֻלָּה לִתְפִלָּה וְנִמְצָא מִתְפַּלֵּל בַּיּוֹם. כִּי תַּנְיָא הַהִיא לַוָּתִיקִין, דְּאָמַר רַבִּי יוֹחָנָן: וָתִיקִין הָיוּ גּוֹמְרִין אוֹתָהּ עִם הָנֵץ הַחַמָּה. וְכֻלֵּי עָלְמָא עַד חֲצוֹת וְתוּ לָא? וְהָאָמַר רַב מָרִי, בְּרֵהּ דְּרַב הוּנָא, בְּרֵהּ דְּרַבִּי יִרְמְיָה בַּר אַבָּא, אָמַר רַבִּי יוֹחָנָן: טָעָה וְלֹא הִתְפַּלֵּל עַרְבִית, מִתְפַּלֵּל בְּשַׁחֲרִית שְׁתַּיִם; שַׁחֲרִית — מִתְפַּלֵּל בְּמִנְחָה שְׁתַּיִם! כֻּלֵּי יוֹמָא מְצַלֵּי וְאָזֵל, עַד חֲצוֹת יָהֲבִי לֵהּ שְׂכַר תְּפִלָּה בִּזְמַנָּהּ, מִכָּאן וְאֵילָךְ שְׂכַר תְּפִלָּה יָהֲבִי לֵהּ, שְׂכַר תְּפִלָּה בִּזְמַנָּהּ לָא יָהֲבִי לֵהּ.

proper time for it [the Sh'ma] is at the rising of the sun, so that the g'ulah* should be followed immediately by the t'fillah, and with the result that the t'fillah will be said in the daytime. That was taught only in reference to the vathikim,** for R. Yochanan said: The vathikim used to conclude it [the Sh'ma] as the sun rose. And may others [delay] till midday, but no longer? Has not R. Mari the son of R. Huna the son of R. Yirmiah b. Abba said in the name of R. Yochanan: If a man erred and did not say the evening t'fillah, he says it [the t'fillah] twice in the morning; [if he erred] in the morning, he says it [the t'fillah] twice in the afternoon? — He may go on praying the whole day. But up to midday he is given the reward for saying the t'fillah in its proper time; thereafter he is given the reward of saying t'fillah, but not of saying t'fillah in its proper time.

---

*The "blessing of redemption" ending with גָּאַל יִשְׂרָאֵל, "Blessed are You, Hashem, who redeemed Israel," which leads from the Sh'ma to the Amidah.
**Literally "ancient ones," suggesting "veterans," observant Jews from an earlier time; primarily it denotes those who were scrupulous and faithful to perform the mitzvoth with alacrity, each at its most appropriate time.

The question was raised: If a man erred and did not say the afternoon t^efillah, may he say it twice in the evening? Should you argue from the fact that if he erred in the evening he prays twice in the morning, [I may reply that] this is because it is all one day, as it is written: *And there was evening and there was morning, one day* (B^ereishith 1:5), but in this case prayer is in the place of sacrifice, and since the day has passed, the sacrifice lapses. Or possibly since prayer is supplication for mercy, a man may go on praying as long as he likes? Come and hear: For R. Huna b. Yehudah said in the name of R. Yitzchak quoting R. Yochanan: If a man erred and did not say the afternoon t^efillah, he says it twice in the evening, and we do not apply here the principle that if the day has passed the sacrifice lapses.

An objection was raised: *Crooked which cannot be made straight and lack which cannot be numbered* (Koheleth 1:15): "Crooked which cannot be made

אִבַּעְיָא לְהוּ: טָעָה וְלֹא הִתְפַּלֵּל מִנְחָה מַהוּ, שֶׁיִּתְפַּלֵּל עַרְבִית שְׁתַּיִם? אִם תִּמְצֵי לוֹמַר: טָעָה וְלֹא הִתְפַּלֵּל עַרְבִית מִתְפַּלֵּל שַׁחֲרִית שְׁתַּיִם — מִשּׁוּם דְּחַד יוֹמָא הוּא,דִּכְתִיב:"וַיְהִי עֶרֶב וַיְהִי בֹקֶר יוֹם אֶחָד". אֲבָל הָכָא — תְּפִלָּה בִּמְקוֹם קָרְבָּן הִיא וְכֵיוָן דְּעָבַר יוֹמוֹ בָּטֵל קָרְבָּנוֹ, אוֹ דִּלְמָא כֵּיוָן דִּצְלוֹתָא רַחֲמֵי הִיא, כָּל אֵימַת דְּבָעֵי מְצַלֵּי וְאָזֵל? תָּא שְׁמַע: דַּאֲמַר רַב הוּנָא בַּר יְהוּדָה, אָמַר רַב יִצְחָק, אָמַר רַבִּי יוֹחָנָן: טָעָה וְלֹא הִתְפַּלֵּל מִנְחָה, מִתְפַּלֵּל עַרְבִית שְׁתַּיִם, וְאֵין בָּזֶה מִשּׁוּם דְּעָבַר יוֹמוֹ בָּטֵל קָרְבָּנוֹ.

מְתִיבִי: "מְעֻוָּת לֹא־יוּכַל לְתְקֹן וְחֶסְרוֹן לֹא־יוּכַל לְהִמָּנוֹת": "מְעֻוָּת.

לֹא־יוּכַל לְתְקֹן״ — זֶה
שֶׁבִּטֵּל קְרִיאַת־שְׁמַע
שֶׁל עַרְבִית וּקְרִיאַת־
שְׁמַע שֶׁל שַׁחֲרִית אוֹ
תְּפִלָּה שֶׁל עַרְבִית אוֹ
תְּפִלָּה שֶׁל שַׁחֲרִית;
״וְחֶסְרוֹן לֹא־יוּכַל
לְהִמָּנוֹת״ — זֶה שֶׁנִּמְנוּ
חֲבֵרָיו לִדְבַר־מִצְוָה,
וְלֹא נִמְנָה עִמָּהֶם.
אָמַר רַבִּי יִצְחָק, אָמַר
רַבִּי יוֹחָנָן: הָכָא בְּמַאי
עָסְקִינָן – שֶׁבִּטֵּל בְּמֵזִיד.
אָמַר רַב אַשִׁי: דַּיְקָא
נַמִּי, דְּקָתָנֵי ״בִּטֵּל״
וְלֹא קָתָנֵי ״טָעָה״.
שְׁמַע מִנַּהּ.

straight" — this applies to one who omitted the Shᵉma of the evening or the Shᵉma of the morning, or the tᵉfillah of the evening or the tᵉfillah of the morning. "And lack which cannot be numbered" — this applies to one whose comrades formed a group to perform a mitzvah and he was not included with them. R. Yitzchak said in the name of R. Yochanan: With what cases are we dealing here? — with one who omitted deliberately. R. Ashi said: The proof of this is that it says "omitted" and it does not say "erred." That proves it.

I. Contradiction between the mishnah and the baraitha concerning the time of תְּפִלַּת הַשַּׁחַר.

  A. *Question*: Our mishnah permits saying the tᵉfillah until חֲצוֹת or שָׁעוֹת ד׳, while the baraitha permits it only at sunrise!

  B. *Answer*: The baraitha is giving the time limit for the וָתִיקִין, while the mishnah is giving it for all other people.

    1. Support for the answer: Rabbi Yochanan also distinguished between the time limit for the וָתִיקִין and that for all other people.

II. Contradiction between the mishnah and Rabbi Yochanan about the final time for תְּפִלַּת הַשַּׁחַר.

   A. *Question*: Our mishnah says that the proper time for the morning t'fillah is until חֲצוֹת or ד' שָׁעוֹת, while Rabbi Yochanan permitted its recitation even at מִנְחָה time in the afternoon!

   B. *Answer*: The mishnah provides the time period within which one is rewarded for reciting the תְּפִלָּה בִּזְמַנָּהּ; Rabbi Yochanan permits a later time in which one can earn the reward for תְּפִלָּה but not for בִּזְמַנָּהּ.

III. Halachic question concerning the מִנְחָה and מַעֲרִיב prayers.

   A. *Question*: May one who did not pray מִנְחָה pray the t'fillah of מַעֲרִיב twice?

      1. The first possibility is that this is not permissible, since the respective times occur on different days.

         (a) The G'mara provides us with support for the fact that a day of 24 hours begins at night according to the Torah.

         (b) The prayers are compared to sacrifices, which may not be brought after the designated day has passed.

      2. A second possibility is that since prayer is merely a supplication for mercy, it is permissible to recite it on the following day.

   B. *Answer*: It is permissible.

      1. Proof is brought from Rabbi Yochanan's statement.

   C. *Question*: Rabbi Yochanan's ruling is disputed: Proof is brought from the baraitha that there is no way to make amends for a תְּפִלַּת מִנְחָה that has been missed.

D. *Answer*: Rabbi Yochanan argues that the baraitha is referring here to someone who missed the מִנְחָה prayer intentionally.

1. Support for Rabbi Yochanan's interpretation of the baraitha is given by Rav Ashi, who points out the usage of the expression בְּטֵל instead of טָעָה in this particular context.

Let us now review the outline of the סֻגְיָא, analyze its components, and take note of the usage of key words:

Part I begins with a רְמִיָּה component, pointing out a contradiction between a mishnah and a baraitha. Even before the contradicting baraitha was cited, we were forewarned to expect the contradiction by the signal word וּרְמִינְהִי. The contradiction is resolved by interpreting the baraitha as referring only to וָתִיקִין, utilizing the principle we learned in the section on background information, that Tannaitic statements may be interpreted to refer to a specific case even though the Tanna, in the interest of brevity, did not so specify. The word תַּנְיָא indicates that the source to be quoted will be a baraitha.

Part II falls into the category of a קַשְׁיָא, challenging Rabbi Yochanan's statement with a deduction from the mishnah. It is answered by a פֵּרוּק of the type that answers the question by interpreting the mishnah so that it does not contradict Rabbi Yochanan. The form of the expression אָמַר רַב מָרִי . . . אָמַר רַבִּי יוֹחָנָן indicates that רַב מָרִי heard the statement directly from Rabbi Yochanan, and we can deduce from the title רַב that he did not receive סְמִיכָה and was therefore probably a Babylonian Amora (as verified in ערובין כ"א), whereas רַבִּי יִרְמְיָה and רַבִּי יוֹחָנָן and בַּר אַבָּא were Amoraim of Eretz Yisrael who did receive סְמִיכָה.

SUGYA ANALYSIS

Part III is a שְׁאֵלָה וּתְשׁוּבָה, with the expression אִבַּעְיָא לְהוֹ notifying us in advance that a halachic question is about to be asked, and indicating that the question was asked by a group of scholars. The answer is introduced by the standard expression of proof תָּא שְׁמַע. Here קֻשְׁיָא וּפֵרוּק are introduced. The question is introduced by the word מֵתִיבִי, indicating that the question is to be from a Tannaitic source, as we might have guessed from the fact that the source is in Hebrew and was asked by a group of people. Rabbi Yochanan's פֵּרוּק receives a סִיּוּעַ from Rav Ashi's דִיּוּק in the baraitha. The baraitha itself is basically הַגָּדָה material, quoting and eluci-dating a verse from Koheleth.

Thus, by examining and analyzing this short סֻגְיָא, we have familiarized ourselves with one of the basic סֻגְיָא outlines which occurs repeatedly throughout the Talmud, in its discussion of various subject matters; we have also gained experience in analyzing many of the סֻגְיָא components and spotted their key words. Some additional important vocabulary expressions that are worth jotting down and memorizing are: הָכָא בְּמַאי עַסְקִינָן; כַּלֵּי עָלְמָא; and שְׁמַע מִנָּה.

Only a few more סֻגְיוֹת need be analyzed thoroughly to complete the student's contact with almost all the basic סֻגְיָא structures, their components, and key expressions. Even in this סֻגְיָא, the signal words and the סֻגְיָא structure could have helped us to comprehend the meaning of the various lines, even if we did not understand all the words and concepts, since we would know when to expect a question, an answer, a proof, etc.

If one continues to learn other סֻגְיוֹת using this process in writing, or at least mentally, he will undoubtedly acquire בע"ה

a reasonable fluency in Gᶜmara comprehension, which will continue to improve relatively rapidly.

An important but often neglected piece of advice offered by the Sages of the Talmud (ערובין נ״ד ב) reminds the student that he hasn't really "learned" a סֻגְיָא and absorbed its details until he has gone over it several times. Even אַהֲרֹן הַכֹּהֵן had to be taught each subject four times by מֹשֶׁה רַבֵּנוּ.

(ועי׳ ספר חיי עולם להגר״י קניבסקי שליט״א, ח״א פי״א)

Students as far back as the time of the Amoraim experienced confusion in their attempts to understand the Gᶜmara, failing to comprehend their teachers' analysis because they overlooked this important aspect of the learning process (תענית ח׳ א). Even after something has been learned, additional repetition of the Gᶜmara to the point where one is capable of reciting all the questions and the answers orally will ensure that the page just learned will remain clear and alive in the memory. Rather than remaining dormant in the back of the mind, the material will be of aid in understanding future סֻגְיוֹת.

(ועי׳ שלחן ערוך הרב, הלכות תלמוד תורה פ״ג, וחוסן יהושע מאמר א׳ פ״ג)

Rules of the Talmud*

Rules of the Mishnah and other Tannaitic sources

1. The Tanna will combine different subjects (a) when they are based on the same preventative enactment (גְּזֵרָה); (b) when they are similar linguistically; or (c) when they are noticed to frequently appear together elsewhere (קכ״ה). Once having mentioned here the law that belongs in a different tractate, he does not repeat it in its own tractate.(כנה״ג פ״ד)

2. A mishnah will repeat previously mentioned information (a) when it is of particular importance to its author; (b) when it has something new to add; (c) for comparison and contrast with other cases; or (d) if it requires a little additional wording. (קכ״ה)

3. Any two subjects mentioned together in a mishnah are to be understood as being similar to one another. (קכ״ה בשם ש״י)

4. The order in which matters are discussed in the mishnah is

*Collected from the writings of רִאשׁוֹנִים and אַחֲרוֹנִים who carefully verified rules used throughout the Talmud. (שארית יוסף=ש״י; כנסת הגדולה=כנה״ג; הליכות עולם=ה״ע; קיצור כללי התלמוד=קכ״ה; שני לוחות הברית=של״ה)

significant. One subject takes precedence over others for one of eight reasons: (a) if it is mentioned explicitly in the Written Torah; (b) if it occurs earlier chronologically; (c) if it is more obligatory; (d) if it is a more general subject rather than a more specific one; (e) if it is more likely to occur; (f) if it occurs more often; (g) if it is simpler; (h) if it is shorter.
(ש״י; עץ חיים)

5. The Tanna sometimes begins by elaborating upon the subject mentioned first in the mishnah, and sometimes he begins with the last subject mentioned. (קכ״ה)

6. At times, a statement made at the end of a mishnah refers not to what was said immediately before it, but rather to the beginning of the mishnah. (ה״ע, ג׳, ב׳)

7. Generally, when a statement is introduced by רַבִּי . . . אָמַר (Rabbi . . . said), this Tanna means to disagree with what has just been said; when it is introduced by the words . . . אָמַר רַבִּי (said Rabbi . . .), he means to support, explain or add to what has already been said.
(כנה״ג ק״א בשם הרא״ש פ״ק דקדושין; מהרח״ש אה״ע ל״ח; ה״ע ב׳, ב׳)

8. When a mishnah cites a difference of opinion on a general subject between two Tannaim, but does not specify which Tanna holds which of the two views, we may assume that the second Tanna holds the stricter opinion. (ה״ע ג׳, ב׳)

9. We are not to interpret that Tannaim are in dispute unless there is an explicit disagreement (כנה״ג בשם מהרי״ק פ״ג). This is the reason why the G'mara always assumes that the mishnah agrees with one of two opinions in a baraitha, and does not say that it represents a third opinion. (ה״ע ב׳, ג׳)

10. If not specified otherwise, the Mishnah generally follows the opinion of Rabbi Meir (the greatest disciple of Rabbi Akiva, and the mentor of Rabbi Yehudah haNasi). The Gᵉmara asks מַאן תַּנָּא (Who is the Tanna—author—of this mishnah?) only when it knows that the particular mishnah was not taught by Rabbi Meir. (אגרת ר' שרירא גאון; קכ"ה; ועי' משנה עדויות א ה, ורמב"ם, הקדמה לפירוש המשנה, למה הוכרו במשנה דעות שאינן להלכה)

11. When the Gᵉmara finds an apparent contradiction in a mishnah, it resolves it in one of two ways: (a) by answering that one part was said by or according to one Tanna, and the other by or according to another Tanna (מִי שֶׁשָּׁנָה זוּ לֹא שָׁנָה זוּ); or (b) by explaining that there is a difference in the cases that accounts for the difference in the rulings. The second way is preferred by the Gᵉmara when possible. (קכ"ה)

12. The Gᵉmara concludes that a mishnah is חַסּוּרֵי מְחַסְּרָא (has some words missing) only if it is obvious from the wording of the mishnah itself. The Gᵉmara, too, will not conclude that the words are missing at the beginning of the mishnah, or that the real meaning in its intended version was the opposite of its meaning in its present version. (קכ"ה; ועי' שם ובשל"ה שני טעמים לזה) (See Section I about חַסּוּרֵי מְחַסְּרָא.)

13. Whenever a mishnah introduces a list of subjects by first giving their number, this has its own significance, for otherwise it need not have been included as we could have counted the subjects ourselves. (ה"ע ג', ב')

14. When a mishnah gives a list of subjects, it often omits some subjects that belong to the list, intending merely to give but a few examples. It does not omit subjects, however, when the list is introduced (a) by וְאֵלּוּ (these are); (b) by a number;

(c) by אֵין בֵּין זֶה לָזֶה אֶלָּא (there is no difference between this and that other than . . .); or in a case where all other matters have been enumerated except for one. (קכ"ה)

15. Sometimes, for reasons of simplicity, the mishnah is inexact concerning an amount or a calculation, when the inaccuracy is לְחֻמְרָא (leaning toward stringency).

(כריתות ה' ב', קכ"ה; ועי' חזון איש או"ח קל"ח)

16. A mishnah sometimes states a law explicitly in its second clause (סֵיפָא) which follows logically from the first clause (רֵישָׁא) even though we could have deduced the law ourselves from the first clause. (קכ"ה)

17. Occasionally Rabbi Yehudah haNasi stated matters in the Mishnah only in order to prevent possible foolish mistakes (כריתות ה', ב', ה"ע ג', ב', מגמ' יבמות נ' א) .(כָּאן שָׁנָה רַבִּי מִשְׁנָה שֶׁאֵינָה צְרִיכָה)

18. Occasionally the Gᵉmara does not accept the reasoning given for an opinion in a mishnah as the major reason, and offers an alternative reason. (קכ"ה מתוס' סוכה כ"ד א ד"ה ר"י)

19. When a baraitha is cited in the course of a discussion, it is given in its entirety even if only one section of it is actually relevant to the question, or leads to a proof which the Gᵉmara wishes to deduce from it. The reason for this is that those who compiled the Gᵉmara decided to record that baraitha in the Talmud for its own sake. (של"ה)

Rules of the Gᵉmara

QUESTIONS

1. Sometimes the Gᵉmara asks a question not based on a mishnah or a baraitha, but simply from generally accepted procedures (מַעֲשִׂים בְּכָל יוֹם). (קכ"ה מתוס' שבת מ"ח א ד"ה מ"ש).

2. In many cases the Gᵉmara asks a question based on an opinion which is not halachically accepted.
(כנה"ג פ"ח משו"ת רשב"א אלף קצ"ט)

3. The Gᵉmara prefers to challenge the statement of an Amora by citing the first part of a mishnah, even if the challenge must be derived by a logical or linguistic deduction, rather than cite a later part of the mishnah, even if that poses a challenge to his statement directly. (כנה"ג ר"ל, ר"י הלוי ס')

4. When a series of questions is asked on an opinion in the Gᵉmara, we can assume that it is the same Amora who asked all the questions, unless there appears a contradiction between the various questions.
(ה"ע ב', ג'; ש"י; ועי' כריתות ה', ג' שסתם קושיא בגמרא היא מרב אשי)

5. The Gᵉmara sometimes asks a series of questions even if the later queries could have been answered with the same answers as the first. The purpose of the later queries is to see whether the Amora being questioned can find a better or more convincing answer. (קכ"ה מתוס' שבת מ"ג א ד"ה כופה)

Some hold that in the original discussion in the beth midrash by the scholars of the Gᵉmara, all the questions were asked consecutively before the single reply was given which resolved them all; but when the discussion was recorded in

the Talmud, the answer was inserted after each question.
(של״ה)

6. The G'mara does not challenge one Amora's statement
with the statement of another, since he has the authority to
differ — except for statements of Rabbi Yochanan, Rav,
Shmuel, Rav Kahana, and Rabba because of their outstanding
scholarship; and except for an Amora's view that was
accepted generally as halachah. Such statements, we find, are
used to challenge another Amora.
(כריתות ה׳, ג׳; קכ״ה; ועי׳ רש״י ב״ק ל״ג)

7. Despite the fact that רַבִּי יוֹחָנָן, חִזְקִיָּה, רַבִּי חִיָּא and רַב were first-
generation Amoraim, they still had the authority to disagree
with Tannaim. Yet the G'mara challenges them with
b'raithoth because halachically an opinion of theirs carries
less weight if contradicted by a baraitha. (קכ״ה)

8. Sometimes the G'mara expresses dismay about a statement
by simply repeating it in bewilderment, as if to say, "What do
you mean by . . ." For example, מִינָא לָךְ מִינָא לָךְ should be read:
"From where do we know . . . ; *From where do we know* . . ?" (*i.e.*
What do you mean by asking that? *or* How could you ask
that?) (של״ה)

ANSWERS

1. Sometimes the G'mara could have given additional answers, but was apparently satisfied with one. (קכ״ה, מזבחים צ״ד, ב׳)

2. At times an Amora asks a question and an Amora of an
earlier generation is quoted as having answered it. What the

G'mara means to say is that the same question was asked in previous generations and was thus answered. (קכ״ה)

3. When we find two conflicting mishnayoth, b'raithoth or סֻגְיוֹת, every effort is made to reconcile them, even with a forced answer. But conflicting statements of two Amoraim are not reconciled with forced answers, since it is a common procedure for Amoraim to disagree. (כנה״ג ק״ח, משפטי שמואל קי״ז)

4. The G'mara does not regard a detail of a story recorded in a mishnah or a baraitha to be insignificant (מַעֲשֶׂה שֶׁהָיָה כָּךְ הָיָה) unless there is no other way to explain it.

(כנה״ג קע״ג מתומת ישרים קמ״ו)

5. A Tanna or Amora who wishes to put forward a new postulate bears the burden of proof; therefore, when he makes a statement or asks a question based on his postulate, even an unlikely alternative interpretation of the two sources he brings is enough to cast doubt upon the validity of his postulate. A forced interpretation or answer may also be used by an Amora in defense of a statement if he is certain it is correct, having received it from a reliable tradition. If, however, he is defending an idea which he originated, he will abandon it if it conflicts with a Tannaitic statement, even if it could have been resolved with a forced answer.

(קכ״ה; ועי' דרכי הגמרא)

THE LANGUAGE OF THE G'MARA

1. At times the same word has different meanings in different places. (כריתות ה', ב'; ה״ע ג', א'; קכ״ה)

2. The word חַיָּב, in most instances, means that the law is

obligatory, but it can occasionally mean that it is merely desirable (לְמִצְוָה). (כריתות ב' ג'; קכ"ה) The word צָרִיךְ is used in connection with an obligation which is only מִדְרַבָּנָן (a Rabbinical enactment). (קכ"ה; ועי' כללי מהרי"ק עמ' ס, א')

3. Sometimes מֻתָּר (permissible) means only permissible as far as one prohibition is concerned, but forbidden because of another prohibition. (קכ"ה)

4. The Gᵉmara often states an exaggerated number, but only when it is more than one hundred. (ה"ע ב', ג'; קכ"ה, מערובין ב' ב וחולין צ' א; ועי' מבוא התלמוד למהר"ץ חיות, ל')

5. The Gᵉmara frequently shortens, extends or changes the order of a mishnah text it is citing, and will shorten even Biblical quotations. (ה"ע ב', ב'; קכ"ה)

MISCELLANEOUS

1. The Gᵉmara will often have a series of unrelated statements recorded only because the same Amora is the source of them all. (ה"ע ב', ב')

2. Rabbinical enactments or edicts (גְּזֵרוֹת חֲכָמִים) should not be compared with one another (to apply details of one to another or to point out contradictions between them; each is an individual matter). (כנה"ג קפ"א בשם רד"ך כ', ח')

3. The rule given in the Gᵉmara אֵין לְמֵדִין מִן הַכְּלָלוֹת (we are not to learn from general rules) (ערובין כ"ז א) applies only (a) when there is some specific reason why a particular case should not be included in the general rule (כנה"ג צ"ה בשם משפטי שמואל); (b) when there are known exceptions to the rule; (c) concerning

rules presented by the Tannaim in which the details of their exact meaning were omitted because of their brevity. (קכ"ה בשם גאון בתשובה)

4. תִּקּוּנֵי סוֹפְרִים ("Scribal emendations"—in Scripture) are not changes in the original text of the Written Torah, but rather interpretations other than the literal meaning, given in consonance with the principle that the Torah expresses hidden ideas in terms simplified for human understanding, just as Scribes might make emendations in their writings for the sake of easier comprehension; and the Sages revealed the hidden meaning of the holy Writ. (קכ"ה; מהר"ל, תפארת ישראל ס"ו;) (של"ה, תושבע"פ, בשם רשב"א ומהרי"ק) The Talmudic interpretation thus reveals a true, valid meaning concealed in the wording of Scripture. (ה"ע; קכ"ה; מהר"ל שם)

5. In matters of דְּרָשׁוֹת and אַגָּדוֹת (homiletical teachings and non-halachic interpretations) an Amora may differ with a Tanna (קכ"ה; אור החיים פ' בראשית) and no ruling obtains as to whose view or teaching is correct. (רמב"ם, פירוש המשנה, סנהדרין פ"י; קכ"ה) [Two Torah scholars—Rabbi Avraham ibn Ezra, (פירוש על התורה) (הקדמה, and Rabbi Moshe Chaim Luzzatto (מאמר על האגדות) —explain that all the opinions and interpretations are true, each portraying or reflecting a different aspect of its subject. (ועי' מכתב מאליהו ח"ג במכתבים, שכתב כן בשם תיקוני זוהר)] Similarly, an Amora may give a reason or source for a law other than the one a Tanna has given, provided there is no practical difference between them. (צל"ח ברכות, בהשמטות; חזון איש, זבחים, לקוטים א', ג')

6. In many cases, for reasons of simplicity, the source of a law is given as one text in the Written Torah, when in reality it may be a different verse. (ה"ע ב', ב')

Rules of Interpretation & Derivation

The following are a few rules about some of the basic methods of derivation from the Torah (הַמִּדּוֹת שֶׁהַתּוֹרָה נִדְרֶשֶׁת בָּהֶן) taken from הליכות עולם שער ג׳:

קַל וָחֹמֶר (*a fortiori*, from the lesser to the greater): Learning the more stringent from the more lenient, based on the logical assumption that if the less stringent law has a certain חֻמְרָא (element of severity), then the more stringent law will certainly have it. And conversely, if a more stringent law has a certain קֻלָּא (element of leniency), then the more lenient law will certainly have it.

1. The קַל וָחֹמֶר can only equate two subjects, but cannot give the subject under study a more extreme קֻלָּא or חֻמְרָא than the source of the קַל וָחֹמֶר. (עי׳ ב״ק כ״ו א)

2. A קַל וָחֹמֶר may be refuted (מְשִׁיבִין עַל קַל וָחֹמֶר) in one of three ways: (a) if in the less stringent law that is our source for the קַל וָחֹמֶר, even one other חֻמְרָא is found, which for some reason cannot apply to the more stringent law (for just as the first law alone has this חֻמְרָא, so it might have the חֻמְרָא we are discussing, as its own special characteristic): אַעְקָרָא דְּדִינָא פִּרְכָא; (b) if a קֻלָּא is found in the more stringent law under study (for just as it has that קֻלָּא even though it is generally more stringent, it might also fail to have the חֻמְרָא we are trying to infer): אַסּוֹף דִּינָא פִּרְכָא; (c) if a third law is found which is also more stringent than the source of the קַל וָחֹמֶר and is known not to have the חֻמְרָא: this is called פִּרְכָא מֵעָלְמָא.

3. When a קַל וָחֹמֶר is refuted by an אַעְקָרָא דְּדִינָא פִּרְכָא, the קַל וָחֹמֶר may be returned to force by citing another lenient law which has the חֻמְרָא that we want to derive, proving that the

prior חֻמְרָא contained in the first source was not the cause of the חֻמְרָא we are discussing.

4. When the קַל וָחֹמֶר is derived from two sources, as in ¶ 3, it may be refuted by a פִּרְכָא כָּלְדְּהוּ, any point that both sources have in common even if it is neither a חֻמְרָא nor a קֻלָּא. But when it is derived from one source it cannot be refuted by a פִּרְכָא כָּלְדְּהוּ.

5. A physical punishment or a warning by the Torah leading to such a punishment may not be inferred through a קַל וָחֹמֶר, but a monetary punishment or a prohibition without punishment may be derived from a קַל וָחֹמֶר. Even a physical punishment may be so derived if the קַל וָחֹמֶר serves merely as a clarification of the meaning of something (גִּלּוּי מִלְתָא).

גְּזֵרָה שָׁוָה Equation of the laws of two precepts, based on identical words in each one's source in the Torah.

1. If neither of the two identical words is used in support of another teaching, no differentiation between the precepts, such as one being more or less stringent, can refute the גְּזֵרָה שָׁוָה.

2. If one of the two identical words is used to support another lesson, the גְּזֵרָה שָׁוָה may be invalidated by the same type of refutation as a קַל וָחֹמֶר (לְמֵדִין וּמְשִׁיבִין).

3. If both words have been utilized in support of other lessons, the גְּזֵרָה שָׁוָה may not be applied at all.

4. Even if the two words are not identical, but their fundamental meaning is the same, they may serve as a basis for a גְּזֵרָה שָׁוָה—for example, וּבָא הַכֹּהֵן and וְשָׁב הַכֹּהֵן—the kohen came, the kohen returned.

5. A קַל וָחֹמֶר argument may be made on one's own responsibility, but a scholar may not postulate a גְּזֵרָה שָׁוָה without

having it by a tradition going back to Moshe Rabbenu. As far as the other מִדּוֹת (rules of interpretation / derivation), Rashi (סוכה ל"א א') holds that they too may not be applied without having them by tradition, as with גְּזֵרָה שָׁוָה; and Tosafoth maintains that they may be postulated on one's own responsibility, as with קַל וָחֹמֶר.

6. A גְּזֵרָה שָׁוָה was not handed down in full detail, but the two words are merely given without specifying which subjects in the Torah are to be linked by them; or sometimes the subjects to be linked were handed down, leaving it to the scholars to seek out the key words that link them. Hence we find arguments in the Talmud about the application of a גְּזֵרָה שָׁוָה.

הֶקֵּשׁ Equation of the laws of two precepts which are mentioned in the same sentence in the (Written) Torah.

1. A הֶקֵּשׁ may not be refuted by noting difference between the subjects, as in a קַל וָחֹמֶר and in types of גְּזֵרָה שָׁוָה, since the equation is considered to have been made explicit by the conjunction.

2. A הֶקֵּשׁ equates in both directions (אֵין הֶקֵּשׁ לְמֶחֱצָה); laws of the first subject may be inferred from the second, and laws of the second from the first.

3. If a הֶקֵּשׁ can be used to teach either a קְלָא or a חֻמְרָא, it is taken to teach the חֻמְרָא, unless it is more reasonable to derive the קְלָא from the הֶקֵּשׁ. (קדושין ל"ד, ב')

4. סְמוּכִים denotes an equation similar to הֶקֵּשׁ, only the subjects being equated are not in the same sentence but in adjacent sentences. The majority of Tannaim use the סְמוּכִים type of derivation, but Rabbi Yehudah does so only under certain circumstances (if it is מֻפְנֶה or מוּכָח; see ד' יבמות).

בְּנְיַן־אָב A "master rule": the Torah gives one example where it applies and intends us to apply it in all other similar cases by comparison. (The literal meaning is "a father-construction" — the source being like a father, אָב, and the cases derived from it, like its descendants.)

1. We sometimes learn such a rule from one source: חֲדָא מַה מָּצִינוּ or בְּנְיַן־אָב מִכָּתוּב אֶחָד or מֵחֲדָא.

2. Occasionally, when some dissimilarity is found in a comparison, it is necessary to derive the בְּנְיַן־אָב from two sources by the same method as a קַל וָחֹמֶר. This process is called a חֲדָא מִתַּרְתֵּי or בְּנְיַן־אָב מִשְּׁנֵי כְתוּבִים.

כְּלָל וּפְרָט A generality followed by a specific term; the rule is then that אֵין בַּכְּלָל אֶלָּא מַה שֶּׁבַּפְּרָט—the generality is limited to only the same situation or law as that which the specific term denotes. The function of the כְּלָל is to prevent us from extending the range of a law beyond the specification by means of one of the methods of derivation.

פְּרָט וּכְלָל A specific term followed by a generality: the rule for it is that נַעֲשָׂה הַכְּלָל מוֹסִיף אַפְּרָט—all that fits into the generality is included. The function of the פְּרָט is to prevent us from limiting the כְּלָל by one of the methods of derivation.

כְּלָל וּפְרָט וּכְלָל A generalization followed by a specific term, which is followed by another generality: then the rule is אִי אַתָּה דָן אֶלָּא כְּעֵין הַפְּרָט—anything similar to the פְּרָט is included, and matters totally dissimilar are excluded (a blending of the two previous rules.)

Some Tannaim and Amoraim interpret general and specific terms by what is called a method of רִבּוּי וּמִעוּט

(עי׳ רש״י סנהדרין מ״ו, א׳, ד״ה כי). In this method, the specific term is seen not as explaining the generalization, as in כְּלָל וּפְרָט, but as limiting it. Consequently, if a generality is followed by a specific term, רִבּוּי וּמִעוּט, the מִעוּט excludes only things which are not similar to the specific term. If the specific term is preceded and followed by a generality, רִבּוּי וּמִעוּט וְרִבּוּי, the מִעוּט merely excludes one item. If the מִעוּט is mentioned before the רִבּוּי, the מִעוּט excludes at least one item.

דְּרָשׁוֹת (literally "searchings, investigations") are based on some irregularity in grammar or word usage which implies to the Sages that there is a deeper meaning which explains the unusual wording (מהר״ל, באר הגולה, באר א׳). In his introduction to סִפְרָא Malbim lists 613 rules of the Hebrew language, and shows that each דְּרָשָׁה stems from a deviation from one of them. The rule that אֵין מִקְרָא יוֹצֵא מִידֵי פְשׁוּטוֹ (שבת ס״ג א) (words of Scripture may not be taken out of their literal context) means only that they are not to be extracted entirely from their textual meaning. However, while they retain their simple meaning, at the same time other lessons may be derived from them (רמב״ן, השגות על סה״מ, שורש ב׳, ד״ה והנה; ה״ע ג׳, ב׳) for the Torah was written with many simultaneously true meanings, just as occasionally in normal conversation statements are made with more than one implication. (שלטי הגבורים, פ״ק דע״ז, עפ״י גמ׳ סנהדרין ל״ד א). When a דְּרָשָׁה is based upon an extra word, only one inference may be made from it, unless two inferences to be made are equally logical, שְׁקוּלִין.

(ה״ע ב׳, ב׳; ועי׳ תוס׳ זבחים ד׳ ב, ותוס׳ הרא״ש ב״ק ג׳, מתי אומרים שקולים)

Precepts in the Torah may not be derived from the words of the Prophets (דִּבְרֵי תוֹרָה מִדִּבְרֵי קַבָּלָה לָא יָלְפִינַן). However, a גִלּוּי מִלְתָא a clarification of the meaning of a verse in the Torah, or